I CANT
BELIEVE
I LIVED
WILD & RAW

By

Stephen Sleboda

Dream Tyger Press
Reisterstown, Maryland
USA

Front Cover Art by Charles P. Hayes
Cover design by Barbara Shaw

ISBN: 978-1-7367739-0-1

Manufactured in the United States of America

10 9 8 7 6 5 4 3 2 1

Dream Tyger Press
Reisterstown, Maryland

Magical Jeep Distributing: www.magicaljeep.com

I CANT
BELIEVE
I LIVED
WILD & RAW

ACKNOWLEDGEMENTS

The poems in this book appeared in the following publications. Grateful acknowledgement is made to the editors of those publications.

Ann Arbor Review
Blue Marble Album
Felt Sun
Holyoke Transcript Telegram
January Review
Minaret
Waterways

Also, my most sincere appreciation to
Alan Britt & Silvia Scheibli for their patience and perseverance,
support and endorsement in all aspects of this project

In brotherhood, through artistic/sacred creative endeavors,
SongsSection collaborator on "Babylon" & "Sir Leonard,"
poet, musician, singer/songwriter teacher & animal rights
activist, Frank Montresor

Photography: Allison Belanger Piscottano & Steve Daboul

Spirit guidance & insights from Danny Shanahan, José Rodeiro
& Steve Barfield

Special thanks to Fred Wolven

The people I want to acknowledge as our lives cross paths are as
follows:
AnnieVCarlyAnnAliceRoseSleboda
Frank Montresor Marta Pelusi Liam Quirk

Steve Barfield Jane Leonard Alan Britt
Silvia Scheibli Charles Hayes Jose Rodeiro
Kath&Brenda Patrick Pontillo Ralph Dolan
Mike Schoenberg TheGoghersSVBPros&Cons
Kyle Wakefield Richard Szydziak
DanielShanahan&CarlaBee
Josef Graham Bob&Mufi Sweet Lorraines
Charlie&Deborah Chet&Sue Roe Allen
Kathy Picard Paul Brown Windy Edick
Dennis BobV Louie JimmyJ Dominico
Esther&Charnae&Destiny Claudia&John
Connie May Fowler Chris Scanlon Picillo
Nico&Kris Paul Roth Fred Wolven
The Brickvilles Chico Greg George&Donna Billy
Halo Friendly Mable Falala Elephants Eye
Less Is More TomorrowsAugust NineMileSky
ThePlague BurntToast BlackEyedSusan The Urges
SaintValentine&TheMassacre FourPlay NedNedskiBand
Nefertiti GreatGrandCanyonIncident TurkeyHillPsalms
Danny&Lati John Shannon & Family
FreaksUnite LightningKellPeteOliBabaTheBest&TheRest
SlebodasQuirksBrennansVanariasVarankas
AuntsUnclesCousinsSignificantOthersNiecesNephews

In Memory:
Mary Eileen Sleboda Mom&Dad
Duane Locke DennisSpencer DannyPetraitis
Frank Wotton Andrew Rosen Doc McHugh
Dave Mackey Kip Picard Al Hurlburt
Ned Lally Roy Pollender John Hebert Ray Ironside

CONTENTS

Part 1

POEMS

Sleep Begins • 3
Excuse Me While I Rake The Sky • 4
Light in Fiery Depths • 5
Ovens of Uncertainty • 6
Sleepwalker Curled into a Cloud • 7
Smoke Fired Sky • 8
Orlena • 9
Nothing to Write • 10
They Once Gave to Blue Sky • 11
Autumnal Golden Moment with Blue Background • 12

Part 2

Shoot the Mothers: #2 Decline of Civilization as Has Been Known
    Or Earth's Last Gasp • 17
Back Home to Her Shell • 21
Pores of Stone • 23
Corrupt Empire • 28
Windows to the Underworld • 29
Culture Shock • 30
Lord Government • 32
Not News and Weather Television Station Nation • 33
Voter Suppression 21st Century Style • 34
The Night the Everything • 35
Bad Rhythm House • 37

Part 3

Blood Moon Time • 41
Is • 42
April Haze • 43
Coeymans-on-Hudson • 44
Simple Note • 45
Piece of Cloth • 47
Toothless Ecstasy • 49
This Is One I'd Never Send • 50
Awake • 51
April Flowers • 52

Part 4

Peaceful Child • 55
Umbrella Vacation • 58
Poem this Way • 59
From the Series: Places of Rest for Body&Soul – Walnut Street • 61
From the Series: Places of Rest for Body&Soul – The Magnolia • 62
Colors of Fall • 63
Down to the Vision • 65
Jacaranda Day • 66
In the Dark • 67
Early Inking • 69
Reason • 71
Gone Thing • 72
Greenside of Wind • 73

Part 5

NEW&OLD Poems

New Moon Morning Looking East • 77
Hearing the Wind • 79
Why is it? - The Leaf Man • 80
If the Eyes Were Not in the Face • 83
Beautiful Gray Day • 84
Some Old Laughter • 86
Wolf Moon of Winter • 87
Strawberry Skyline • 88
She said, "Jesus Loves You" • 90
Oh America • 92
Ride the Thermals • 93
Order of The Calendar • 95
Good Morning Wind • 96
Graceful as Sun Warms • 98
How Proud, Poor Pitiful Amerika • 99

Part 6

LITTLE BELL SERIES INTERLUDE

Little Bell #4 • 105
Little Bell #7 • 106
Little Bell #8 • 107
Little Bell #9 • 108
Little Bell #12 • 109
Little Bell #16 • 110
Little Bell #18 • 111
Little Bell #20 • 112

Part 7

SONGS

Babylon • 115
Sound of the World • 120
CW Jones • 121
Full of Bones • 123
Falling in Love with a Statue • 125
Grass Is Always Greener • 127
Find Someone it might be You • 128
Edge of the World • 130
You Saw Him Singing • 131
Sir Leonard • 133
Buddha & the Belle • 137
Mister Secrets • 139
Her Blessings • 140
Mary Eileen • 141
The Old Irish Woman • 142
Here Comes the Wintertime • 143
Moonlight Serenade • 144
Still Sing Now • 145
Mental Institution • 146
Bourgeois Heaven • 148
Green Frog Skin Garden • 149
Vagabond Villa • 150

Credits • 153
Poet's Biography • 155
Publications • 157
Testimonials • 159

1

Think in the morning, Act in the afternoon,

Eat in the evening, Sleep in the night

William Blake

SLEEP BEGINS

Early star like an ornament
on an oak tree limb

Flashing lights from a plane
through a stand of pines

Sunset below a mottled sky path,
crosses the street

I hear the usual dim shades fall
Thinking bursts into crumbs

Black squirrel scurries by
jumps, turns and climbs,

The ornament now, a nest,
sleep begins, tail across tiny cold face

EXCUSE ME WHILE I RAKE THE SKY!

    Eyelashes of dusk
rake silence
        from sky,
motor noise gurgles,
 ears shut tight,
A formation of
        Catalpa green
      proceeds
            in the direction
where wind always blows

LIGHT IN FIERY DEPTHS

The charter is received today.
It looked like spaghetti and sleet.
I wanted to write a name
as if someone might understand.
Instead it was easier
to grow feathers
and pretend about a dream
in an attic.
Voices screamed, and when
burning cauldrons
entwined into swirls of
fiery depths where fears
waited on shoulders,
the search began
for a man-made instance
covered under
fingers of black fuel oil,
fully equipt to toss
regrets into
a chlorine-filled pool.
The smiles, rotted teeth from
yellow and brown bits of tobacco,
laughter and an odd sound
from a garden hose nearby
merged into a nightmare
that remained barely afloat yet
vaguely in tune.
At this juncture
it became clear
this celebration of standards
was meant to fit
everyone's idea of popular.

OVENS OF UNCERTAINTY

The weather channel
could change direction
and become wolf eyes.

Tears might symbolize rain.
Pups play in puddles.

The instant imagination
folded and became reason
all hell broke loose.

The carnival lost its wheels.
Now flooded, they travel with marbles
of lost children
on muddy streets
dormant hemisphere
sacred robes.

I called out to administration:
"the pie doesn't taste like food,"
"I need more barn,"
the musician claimed,
"I need more barn!"
"The pie doesn't taste like food."

Ovens of uncertainty
blame imagination
while country
cooks itself
in its own oils.

SLEEPWALKERS CURLED
INTO A CLOUD

In the bishop's hour
ready to extinguish
relics in thoughts of dream,
tongue, eyelash
lip, teeth
muscle and bone,
sleepwalkers
curled into a cloud,
arms bereavement-like
in charge of dismay
in search of glare
near the seasonal cycle
repositioned
to dismiss
an oncoming storm,
candles farewell.

SMOKE FIRED SKY

Village scene unfurls
his arm tied
behind her
barking dog
being settled where
grief awaits their
common garden
to kneel
like rain pressed
against sacred ground

Night and day
Moon with Sun
Lost Stars
upside down
spill droplets of truth
near gray wolf scent
at rest under
smoke fired sky

ORLENA

An old girlfriend
blew in from
Long Island Sound,
she says her name is Orlena
but I know her better as Pam.

She had silk sheets
and a Cadillac boy
named Dan.

I pulled up the curtain
at her debut and they cut my salary
and ran me outta town.

Oh, come down easy Orlena
Come down easy Pam
You'll always be a star
I'll always be your man.

NOTHING TO WRITE

Nothing to write
without a pen
Never mind
without a hand.

The pulpit won't hold
another summer of dust.
Take it out back
throw it over the rail
see if it grows wings.

Find another place
to dream
like sounds
in rolling hills
made green around each bend
across the pulse of neutron stars.

Maybe open a piece
of mail
meant for scissors and glass.

Scratch sidewalks
with alphabets
lost children memorized
to forget their names.
Where chalk on
a teacher's stone reads
'Here lies nobody.'

THEY ONCE GAVE TO BLUE SKY

For once I thought about all the bodies,
not in a morbid way
but like life
they once gave blue sky,

vegetation, clear water, vast tracks of land,
and wind blowing from screen window
to screen window and room to room in houses
through hallways from north to south

and through the woods out back or out front
whichever was front or whichever was back
maybe on what neighbors misplaced packages
or where numbers were placed either on or near
the door, maybe nailed, tacked, taped or hung,
probably black like
an old hairbrush under tissue in a wastebasket

left there by mistake like it never mattered in
the first place.

AUTUMNAL GOLDEN MOMENT
WITH BLUE BACKGROUND

Golden
needles
come
into
view
where
unfound
rain
like
blinds
dodge
jays
danger
calls,
black
tail
squirrel
caution
glares
and
an
instance
of
sunlight
on
its
return
to
the
welcome
mat

bark
of
a
pine
tree
stand.

2

The carriages splintered into pieces,
war destroyed doorways and walls,
the city was a fistful of ashes,
all the dresses shivered into dust…

–Pablo Neruda

SHOOT THE MOTHERS: #2 DECLINE OF CIVILIZATION AS HAS BEEN KNOWN OR EARTH'S LAST GASP

And it's shoot
the mothers!
Detain
any troublers,
face-masked brothers
ready to brawl at the drop of
Molotov cocktails,
long guns loaded that
hang on shoulders,
images quick to
raise the tempers
and lost are all
the fathers
in their suburban
druthers where
peacekeepers
reflect all those
random murders,

graffiti culture
above all other,
a time for
war if there
ever was one.
Push down
gas-masked soldiers
by unauthorized
marauders,
take to the
streets of Amerikakaka
burning.

The changing times,
the mumble-filled
anthems,
take to bended
knees like fashion-wave
hypesters.

Insurgents of disturbance,
reckless &
twenty-four hour
rule of law,
global pandemic,
soothsayer republic,
pardon me mister
where is the sisterhood
black lives matter?

Swallowed whole
in media-belly,
bloated from
reactionary focus.
Bloodied nightstick
swashbucklers,
steam-fed federales,
stomped down
on tar and
shot down with
maimed-like precision.

The decision
is yours
on the couch

at the country-club
disgust fest.
Full & sore &
annoyed & deployed
in scapegoat-syndrome rhythm,
to release tension,
from central
rant free
rattle storm
bench press incisions.

Troopsters and tricksters
mismatched &
plague-smashed like
cold hearted orbs
& metal detector
grinder mashers.
Home,
home on
the silent
lip range
rule reincarnations.

No more
God's glory,
no more
heaven's centuries.
Does this say
anything at all
when the moon
& it's hotter,
the cold

& it's wetter
along
ammunition highway
lie skeletons
of here afters?

And over and
over goes under
& turn away
cryptic-gilded-plunder,
all goes at
the red light
& lets the
one-if-by-land,
two-if-by-sea;
stop, where
three,
two, one,
blasts off
to the sun.

BACK HOME
TO HER SHELL

The snows filled in
between the dots

We said what we meant
as fragrance from
heaven was passing by

on its way to war
past the hardcore sound
of a broken heart

and it shattered
right there on the
century in front of itself

and after all
the awards
from time
with glam & glory

while the ministries
aligned like magnets
where numerals
mattered more
than the count at the
end of the hall

And this all
coiled to keep
from the cold
as nothing but sighs
in a beggars bowl,

cloth hat,
wool sock
copper, lint,
and the reflection
of another leather strap
beating a dead horse
like a victory drum roll
on the way
back home
to her shell.

PORES OF STONE

Jaded vile
cadenza,
sleek & storied
ticket-taker
at the
20th century porno
movie theater
in downtown
Eraserville USA,

tobacco
in the air,
jumble mumble
profit from the cans
falling from
the pocket peoples
purple eater,

a nickel
covered in spit,
everywhere
it's showing
the exhibition
under the heavens,
screaming expletives,
like a bullet-voice
wheezing-whine,

the tack
between
big and little toes
all crusty, clammy,

all dirt and lint and
skin made from
foster children's rhymes.

Dead air rushing
from armpit hair
welcoming the inner child
to a niche-filled
seat beside
a big bowl of
savage stew.

Gobble down
the crumbs &
slurp venom
off the spoon,
midnight has
a giftcard &
awaits the sound

from keys at
the back door &
awaits with chocolate
covered nightmares;
under the pillow,
under the bag lady
luggage & linens
soiled from a night
on the grate
air blowing back
matted
gray white hair.

Scream the
gravel-gasp growl,
each pebble
carefully placed
beside & behind
floppy red tongue-tied
hangers on

where deer turn
in time to play
ring around
the fabrication
wind turbine nation.

Dance the ring around
the nape of
the necklace place,
vacant
like the store
it came from
after the
third hurricane
hit the coast
that year;

like magic,
everybody packed
up their bad teeth,
left everything behind,

every bug that
ever crawled
across bed sheets,

blankets and pillows,
bloody and black
like a night
that wouldn't stop
being dark,

that wouldn't
hold hands and
bring force
to push into
that ladle mouth
and watch
sounds that
sing between
silver and cold,
silver and gold,

peaceful and graceful,
sinful and rolled
up in a
sleeping bag,
crazed eyes
withdrawn into
flesh-full sockets,
fresh from
leather book's promise
stammering along
the lonely land.

This page
goes on
for two days,

this page
goes on
for three
in the 2011 raft
weary-bumpy
road explosion
explanation &
bitter tragic invasions,
chemical-laced
abrasions &
double-talk reincarnations;
incantations from
the pit of the restless
karmic calendar
fallen off
the door &
like the
cold body
of an
orange room,
matted to soft words
and a thousand
pores of stone.

CORRUPT EMPIRE

Here are the terms.
Death. Death. Death. Death.
There is no room left for life.

The bully mentality laughs
        at Mother Earth.
Her sincerity, patience and stamina
    pause long enough, then blood.

Her son won't hold her in his arm.
    She cries herself to sleep
            at night.

He has trained himself
    to dismiss soul.

A bouquet of flowers grows
alongside the reservoir road.
    No vase, no lips to kiss.

    Corrupt Empire
    turns from feeling.
Warriors heavy with peace
        water the sky

WINDOWS TO THE UNDERWORLD

What kind of a poem am I supposed to write filled with broken glass from the windows of the underworld? Arm all scarred from gnawing at the bone, tearing of flesh, eyes ripped from their sockets for dessert, dictionary definitions of satanic worship. Right field coach? Let me start today's game. The glove fits this small left hand even though neither foot reaches the ground from the end of this first base bench languishing next to an overrun trash can of bees. The sun is made of fingernail polish and right field faces west. I'm an infielder but I'll play outfield. Nobody knew the coach was psychotic or the kid was adopted. Good luck when you're blinded in right field master infielder. Nothing attracts the scent of blood more to Mammon than grandmother's gnarly fingernails.

CULTURE SHOCK

Night
sticks
turn
to
prayer beads

fill
eye
sockets
of
ghost dancers

float
past
midnight

gasps
for
breath

on
any avenue
called
home.

This battering
bone
now broken
and thrown

lands
ready
to
nest

in
the
depths
of
fire, in water.

LORD GOVERNMENT

Disturbance alert words
    like collage art
        or an animated
commercial on television
    where even the fake smiles
        and seven syllable laughter
            go haywire.
Humanity melts into puddles &
scavengers sip from the pools.
Suddenly a Christmas wreathe
            has meaning
        like a high wire act
            across Texas Ranger
                territory with
    a couple decades of
        legalization plans
                in the trunk.
Take your pick, pot, people,
        plastic fantastic
                forgone convulsions.
It certainly does not matter
        what these words mean.
Ask any run-of-the-mill scholar
        or an insurgent
            up on sedition charges,
                rank and file.
        Home home on the bone,
        surely by granting allegiance
                to the latest caper
Lord government has concocted
        to wage, end or begin war,
        a shiny new truck and pension
                will align with this
                twisted capitalistic scam

NOT NEWS & WEATHER TELEVISION
STATION NATION

Bullets
given for
protection
from a
windstorm
in Colorado,
a miracle in Pennsylvania,
newsworthy stories of
Seminole County crazies,
added up
& the mill closed.

The move to Tennessee left weather
to bring rain where
there was none.
A lot of rain.

A drop or two on a crumpled leaf
by a path near a deer run
was plenty to keep
the dream alive.

All held hands,
danced in a square,
sang ritual government songs,
fused commercialism & sensationalism,
knew nothing about socialism, communism & complained
crusty old angry white men
& young controlling brown immigrant women
were not
at a party
with a funny looking boss that
refused to buy a mask!

VOTER SUPPRESSION 21ST CENTURY STYLE

Voter suppression Twenty-First Century style
Knock knockin
on the governor's door.
Looks like that government
building is one the latest
swath of tornadoes
left standing this time.
Who's behind that door?
Who's being lead back
into the end of the world as we know it?
Grandfather, why are all those
big boys in blue
rough and tumble
leading that State Representative
of grace & dignity
down the hallway
in handcuffs, out the door & under arrest?
Does it have something to do with freedom?
In our country during these days
criminals have handcuffs.
And are arresting Lawmakers!
And as long as everyone just
does as they are told
And doesn't make trouble
And lets domestic terrorism
reign supreme
Everything will be just peachy!

THE NIGHT THE EVERYTHING

The night, the
everything, made
from the
molten of Hades

At nine o'clock
ever and always
stopped like
the lips of the
forlorn maiden

The need for heroes
slipped past
the hiding place,
perhaps void of sense
maybe drugged,
or in an ordinary dream state
wedged between
the goal posts

She was the tiniest
of dancers
at the edge of the stage,
star struck,
gown flowing,
eyes alive in the
spirit of the venom
pouring forth

Always the bell,
always the cellar,
and secret passage

and the song of the world
about to explode

The great experiment
churning below
under even the lowest of floors
The song trilled
out in an explosion
of lost fire,
voices huddled
together and the
mirrors and the mask
collapsed into
musings of an
angry mob,
furious and
feasting
at the altars
of insurrection.

BAD RHYTHM HOUSE

Bad rhythm house on the square
No noise, nobody there
Ancient burial site
Bones the size of clipped fingernails

Someone please hand out
A handbook to move past
To confirm theory
To touch flame
To burn burn rain off the stove

Seismic meter wants to dance
Sing to butterflies & bats in their trance
No one moves, is anything said?
A bundle of nothing
In the weatherworn shed

Carried out the bodies in canvas bags
Layered in freezer trucks piled four high
A war began
Silence made a stand
The promise of love
Was an excruciating pain
Lost in Exnamelessville.

3

With the ghostly shapes of dead heroes
Moon, you fill
The growing silence of the forest

–Georg Trakl

BLOOD MOON TIME

Blood moon
misty morning stand
beside pine tree
crawling
in absent sun.

Excuse
whispers
from wind.

Darkness
in my hand
a gift for you
to write or tie
old ribbon
where our
box was left
to water
gardens
for bleached sky.

All aboard
cold carpets
trumpet
sighs.

Now is when only time
moves empty grief sublime.

IS

He is not
There was nothing
I said
There was another
She sighed
There by the door

The broken
He filled
The collapsed
I said
She stood
The wind

APRIL HAZE

Lunar cycle
  warm
 April haze

Right shoulder
  pasted
   to midnight

Blue like
  the name
   of my
    name

Cross
  pointed
   inward

Footpath
    headed
      south

Breathe spiral
    silence

Light your
   voice,
    our
   darkness

Enter within, the way out.

COEYMANS-ON-HUDSON

for Charles P. Hayes

How would it say,
"Hay, Hudson here!"

All these speed boats,
party boats,
while azure, crimson and ivory
sink flat like old noodles in a pot.
Winds wait on a light
to turn green!
Green, green, beautiful green.

The Hudson still has no name
all these years later.
We meet where
memory brings
all feet inside
a porch where
lizards flash
upon her paint-chipped wooden gate.

A barge awash
in awkward gray robe
stumbles by
drowns out conversation
about normality, kayaks and
adjustable mask replacements.

A SIMPLE NOTE

A simple note
from the heart
of the world

Sent like snow
to cover the wound,
a severing gash,
blemish or mole

Gnashing
like a load of
old cities
in a dream soaked
night

On the cold plot
where the red carpet
lead to the
story of morning & mint

Faded purple shawl
on that
wild blindful wind

Charred countryside
scorched and severed
any notion
that every color will do

Burning heart, buried love
cleansed in fire
free once more

Drenched in silence
like the question
             it was meant
                  to be

PIECE OF CLOTH

A piece of cloth
on table sunlight
feather falls
in that feather-fall way
Across & under
just missing each turn
toward cold, wet & air we breathe

Sorrow & her sister, blue sky
welcome green grass shapes,
hands that stop &
start & ring weather
from her hair

On the mantle
a picture in a warm place,
a home where the Riverside club
came one by one
to the screen door out back,
maybe for scraps, pennies or an
infectious smile,
the lecture too about
keeping out of sight.
like a generation
in time of worry
fear and fortitude
stuck in the throat.

On an old muddy path
winding through a patch of woods
a race begins
nobody needs to win.

Nobody even needs to run;
the river will do
that for us.

Water will flow,
morning will bring its dream
like someone's song about love,
someone who knew
how much heart
it took to
fill the jug &
pass it on
like lightning
on a hill,
rain in the fires eye,
the shifting
shape of
wind.

Was it all a magic trick?
Could it even be called
evening when sun set?

TOOTHLESS ECSTASY

Pits of the lawn
behind the hemlock row
grow grow!

Do what gets said
and not what is thrown
grow grow grow.

Establish a home
deep in yourself
someone you'll know!

THIS IS ONE I'D NEVER SEND

The Muse is here
as if it's a her
she'd say it's a hymn
to get pen
and be placed
in light.
Do what you're told.
Never mind what rhymes.
Shoulder hip teeth toe
Rhythm and row
row boat across foam.
The line at wisdom is long.
Bring along who you can
sullen dream
filled with foes.
A bell to ring.
Breath to breathe.
Rain and snow
Sad masses
donate woes.
Armed with lemmings
and over they go.
Armed for
portions of freedom,
fly away like a world
in a breadline below.
Our world I was told
Until I knew it was no.
Streetlights vanished.
Spotlights overgrown.
Cry out fear
Point to song
The Muse is here
Nowhere to go.

AWAKE

Awake is done better asleep,
full scale drain gutter
interference alliance chasm.

In about one more windy day
pains here and in between sky blue
and white clouds will bleed.

Have no representation without
electric shock treatment memory
in some form of a back pocket.

When walking across the street
the straight hat gathers sticks.
Other than sun, moon has a cheek.

Spring is in the hair, green goblet
in the next minute, a blossom
on the new deck, the mother who cries,

this is all part of the plan
like a soiled shirt in a pile,
a penny, a fortune teller prophecy.

Just imagine how the next word starts
and in frogs you trust to your night.
Sit by the old wall discolored

and the thought-meaning was easy,
The nakedness of not known, not weather
intersection on a map in her dream.

APRIL FLOWERS

April became the ear of an apparition
filmed where spotlit yard

dogs heard backhoes when
people painting fingers paddled eyes

in ventriloquists cabins near rivers
for war was a reminder

mouths full shiny and gloss-stained
spewed glamour from crackled lung

money necessary to keep this
leisure flame burning body after body.

4

There is a sorrow here that doesn't
call itself that

–Tomas Tranströmer

PEACEFUL CHILD
for Frank Wotton

When the train derails:
inspectors, first responders,
authority-fueled officials,
tactical research and
restoration team leaders,
security-garbed
credential-laden
buttoned down
micro-managed
affiliate board associates
and coordinators
descend upon the wreck
where: wallets,
packets with
unfamiliar markings,
chairs, staples, paper clips,
cardboard boxes,
folders & tacks,
laptops, cellphones,
coffee cups
& other familiar
furniture fragments,
clothing too and shoes,
watches, rings,
roses & wine bottles
have been strewn about.

There are other items
hidden where
evidence could easily
be mistaken
for Trip Tix to Disney World
in the spring.

And objects
under broken pieces
of twisted
and dismantled iron
recognizable only
by the light of day,
that remains
absent now,
and
on its own
crash course
with reality
thousands of miles
to the west.

Then the bodies
begin to reveal
themselves:
wild eyes,
broken noses,
collapsed lungs,
infrared & underfoot,
yet one
has this look
never seen before,
a peaceful,
child-like gaze
enveloped in
the spirit-world,
already on the way,
leaving troubles & worries
in its wake,
on muddy and

rubble-filled footpaths
alongside
the murky runoff
from the
hillside above
& the storm that
moved east
overnight.

UMBRELLA VACATION

Jesus under
Mateus bottles
in a garage
with one wall missing
Front lawn fire
Authorities and a
pearl handled
Saturday night special
where floorboards creak

The porthole window
from the rusted bathtub
to the alleyway
and stone table in between
like an umbrella vacation
on the ivory sands of hell

Frenzy full with foam and bones
cries the mentor
from a cabin-stained soul
released from prison
behind bars
for crimes
only the rabid beast
would commit
with play get out of jail
cards free scattered
from smoke to ground

POEM
THIS
WAY

I
wanted
to
write
a
poem
down
the
page
like
Hayes
used
to
do
and
the
Alligator
also
made
it's
way
this
way
in
the
early
days
before
Pop
needed

his
Geriatric
piss
bottle
emptied.

From the Series:
Places of Rest for Body & Soul

WALNUT STREET

Walnut street stroller
   wheels and bricks of summer
All the imagination
   at the bottom
 of the stairs.
    The sun was life
 and the sky was alive!
  The availability of sound
        from weeds
       through cracks
  in the wooden gate
left like a masterpiece
   no one would touch.
  Tiny fingers stretched,
     reached, curled
     from the shade
          beneath
        the awning
     as it rolled into
   the bliss it called itself.

THE MAGNOLIA

for Mom & Dad

Maple tree blues harp 'Swing Low Sweet Chariot'
and the big black car
round top from the underworld.
King Deer and mountain cliff,
the highway, her dark soul,
lines in the sky.
The way home, no way home.

Front porch and radio vines
Fever, the taste of death,
lawn chair assassin
wear the coat, the tie.
Backyard memory, cement smile
dandelion, lilacs and clover.

Dining room table,
mantle paint brown
three windows,
take apart the cabinet,
silver ladder
crib and child
cries for mother
on Magnolia dawn summer.

COLORS OF FALL

Nothing to remember
about words or either eye.

Not like losing JFK
when early dismissal came

and walking home alone

on a cloudy day
down Franklin street

thinking about snow &
sliding on our shoes

down the water drainage slide

But only autumnal cold
maybe running home &

the hat that didn't fit
this frightening fall

being jarred free
from a fortress
off the highway
under some tree
down the ladder
into a secret place
only thoughts found

Always ended up

in the tobacco room,
In the alcohol room,
In the lipstick room
with sparkling jewels,
finger rings,
bracelets & furs

DOWN TO THE VISION

for Duane Locke & Jane Leonard

Then there was that time
down in Ybor City
Or maybe Davis Island
in a ray-glo rubber room rhyme
When the notion
to take hold of Astral Physics

On the red sweater nurse
with shiny wine nails
spilled out of the play time
locked ward floor.

Cozy as it was in the open door closet
The whistle blew and blew and
blew in the unarmed guards.
And from the strong armed rescue
With the day room parachute in mind

that lead down to the Vision
And how we'll all get off
holding on to the dirty-white
raggedy robe to leave this world,
to leave this age.

Just maybe for an open space
where the cities glare,
wisdom gloom standards and factions
and ready-made dreams,
dance with laughter, even,
peace and quiet at ease.

JACARANDA DAY
>for the Immanentists

Fire ants and cement steps
side doors locked
where curtains blew in
termite speckled forms.
The scent of some other scream
over the refrigerator
on the mattress up each stair,
Jacaranda day,
distemper year,
crawl space movement,
I heard someone dream.
Inside out flower
stallion upside down
curdled words
desert black
champion storm
mint trilled night
severed song

IN THE DARK

for Alano

The two-wick candle full
of past voices
whispers between it's flickering light.

Do not despair, the language
you thought was yours
turns out to have it's beginnings
buried amongst pine cones
under the footpath that stopped
at One Sacred Burial Site.

Water, wind-sun, breathe-earth
is all you'll need.

Blindness has returned.
It wants to hold your hand,
the one with the scar,
from night
full like a plate
glass window.

The nightmare three score
years behind the memory of
the body in the attic
only sleep would welcome.

The attic
in a house on
a street named
after a tree
with roots in
cold ground where

to be a pebble
only brought
more
sound,
darkness and
like thunder that
sways with hesitation
into a hidden place,
fills
past voices
with whispers to
candlelight.

EARLY
INKING

Turn that
storage unit off!

Turn the
Black Moon on!!

Any words
will do

when bad poetry
is on the menu.

Look at
none of
those people

who need to
get busy

with
mathematics.

Fill up the truck
with accountants,
statisticians,
micro managers
and recovery coaches.

How many gridirons
can fill up
our country

before bombs go
bursting in thin air?

This page
is too small
to fit this inking.

REASON

Put down the reason.
Make a list for life.
Think about the color black.
Call the sun an animal.

Present anyone with anything.
Find a blue cloud, make it rain.
Stand next to the end of the world.
Chisel God next to an elevator number.

Remember the hour you were born.
Sing a song about number zero.
Disregard every voice that says, 'the.'
When it's over reach for the flower.

Something never began.
Grass grew but not green.
In came the rest of the herd
as if a world grew water.

Air pulled decency over eyes.
Here, the talk about reason
like an opening in the earth
big enough to rename a pebble.

GONE THING

The steps that ache.
Insects and other
Bumps that go thing
In the night.
Moon as bright as blue.

GREEN SIDE OF WIND

Oh spiral mist,
friend of language
tending an obsession,
you give so freely
a morning of laughter
speeding behind
a green side of wind
yet rest and
huddle beside
breath-filled voices
of sand
and sunlight
upon the
rocky coast.

5

He wants to break into the bank,
rob clouds, stars, gold comets,
and to buy what is hardest to get:
the sky.
And the man is dead.

–Rafael Alberti

NEW MOON MORNING LOOKING EAST

Morning Looking East
L
o
o
k
I
n
g
East
Oak
a
n
d
Pine
Get
Along
S
o
C
a
n
W
e

I agree like a tree,
stand straight, tall,
hold out my leaves

in spring
ready
to receive.

Thank you
sun
dew
earth
song.

We
are
here
for
you
when
ready
to
follow
our
silence
our
calm.

HEARING THE WIND

Hearing the wind
doesn't mean
trees will fall
on the house or
death will carry my soul
to the room
of fiery screaming voices
swirling downward
into the abyss.
A flower may just as well land
on our welcome mat.
Unless the wind has blown it away.
Why, the mat of course!
The flower has other stops
to make along its way today.

WHY IS IT? - THE LEAF MAN

Why is it?
When I wake up
I gotta crawl
Out of my head.
Why is it?
When I wake up
I can never
Make my bed.

Why is it?
When I put my rake on
I'm the leaf man,
Deep into the ground
I'm the leaf man,
In search of
Never sound.

Why is it?
Why is it all around?
Why is it?
When it's dark inside
I never see the light.
Why is it?
When it's dark inside
I never know
If it's the night.

Do you want to know
Where I stand with the issues?
Do you want to know
When I sleep with the tissues?

Do you want to know
The substance that I misuse
Do you want to know

The dream where I don't lose
The that that I won't choose
The sleep that I call booze
The drink when I call snooze?

Why is it?
When I put my rake on
I'm the leaf man.
Is it?
When I put my rake on
I'm the leaf man,
In search of
Solid ground.

Why is it?
Why is it always round?
Why why why,
Why why why why,
Seven times I said it
Maybe now I'll bleed it
I'll probably never
Read it
If it's food
Would I eat it?

Why is it?
Why is it?
Why is it is it?

Why is it?
Why is it?
Why is it is it?

Why is it?
When the curse hits
I never can escape it.
Why is it?
When the curse hits
I can't
Get my cape to fit it.

I'm the leaf man,
When I put my rake on
I'm the leaf man.
When I put my rake on,
Dormant in the cold,
Layin' around,
Why is it?
Why is it?
Ground down sound.

IF THE EYES WERE NOT IN THE FACE

If
the
eyes
were
not
in
the
face
but in another fortress of the body
perhaps
on
the
balls
of
the
feet
to keep a hold of Mother Earth
maybe
we
would
not
have
to
rise
above
clouds
to
plant
flagpoles
on
the
moon

BEAUTIFUL GRAY DAY

Beautiful gray day
appears
with
sun
splatters
from
west
to
east
across cream
colored walls,
clutter-filled,
flames
claiming
songs
by
Trakl,
calling
out
Neruda
in
a
room
where
light
tied
to
a
kite
string
flies
like an

owl
out
of
tall
pines
through
dusks
emerald
eyes!

SOME OLD LAUGHTER

In a damp closet
hung some old laughter
i tore a strand down and
brought it to the bank
to put in my account
the banker began crying and
i was ushered from the premises
they kept the laughter and
told me it would gain interest
in no time I would be able to buy
a car, a house, maybe even
start my own business
i could send all my children
to college and they could become
poets and artists and musicians and
when they graduated they could
return to the bank and
withdraw that piece of laughter and
hang it back in the closet where it belongs

WOLF MOON OF WINTER

Oh my, shaking of the core

Bleeding from wounds of reverend wake-up.

Give me an amen!

And a bell barely rung next to your name

Silence of austerity

Climbing walls of the republic.

Freshly washed hair blowin in the breeze

Wolf moon of winter open your eyes.

STRAWBERRY SKYLINE

by Patrick Pontillo/Stephen Sleboda

The ace of spades held deeply within a conspiratorial sleeve
floated downward, through the mass of clouds
that pushed the continental plates of a strawberry skyline
into a dark gravity that once held the moon over an ocean's balcony.

Maps lay frozen under camps of the enemy where friendly fire grew wings.
Spotted birds deliver hard tack bread to ancestors as they weep tears of
     frayed greenery.
Courage scampers across borders of arrogance, in pockets of disgust &
     fame.
There was a sound coming from the well, along with light only crickets
     knew.

Tracer bullets at midnight. Then pistols at dawn, followed by flash bulbs
     firing off
in minds of survivors who see encores of tragedy in a theater of fear.
A distant solitary planet, posing as a star, clears a granulated sky
during another cricketless night.

There are no borders to conceal the glow coming from the starless
     distance.
Energy given to language where voice is a sand dune
and thought has no spike under its tongue, grapples with the snail in the
     mirror.

Gravity looks back toward the scene of an accident where,
within its perimeters, rain puddles reflect the pulsation of red lights.
Everyone crosses the Do Not Cross line in a disheveled motion
that resembles a mud dried trench coat which once sat under a Christmas
     tree,
wrapped nicely in a department store box with matching ribbons and
     bows.

The owl lands in an oak darkening the memory of cloth.
Trying to find a priest in this century is forbidden and will
    not be tolerated.
Deliveries to the warehouse startle the innocent one.
Let's call it a day and welcome homeless a new generation of
    dissonant strangers.

SHE SAID, "JESUS LOVES YOU"

What should I know
to hear the eagle soar
to watch the flower bloom
to see the spider spin
to catch rain
to hold air
to smell freshly cut grass
to crawl inside clear blue sky
to wander with clouds?
Should I know people play mind games?
Should I know what symbolizes what?
I know the sun when it sifts through the sky.
I know that is the sun.
It's not a symbol for happiness,
just as I am not a falling star.
To be a falling star
crashing through the dark
only the watchers will catch
splitting the leaves
diving for pearls with an invisible string.
What should I know to lie upon
the cool earth
to touch a breath of autumn
in New England?
Should I know a dim lit jammed freeway
means sickness and hate?
Should I know a mysteriously dark alley
means a gunshot through my heart?
What should I know
as the sparrows bubble up from the grasses
as the lizards dash across the sidewalk
stopping only for an occasional nod?
What should I know

when I hear music curl out of drainpipes?
When I see darkness as darkness
should I know I could die any minute?
Any minute is the same
as the minute I was born.
Should I hear those footsteps
to be the blood stained body
I saw on the television last year?
Should I know all these things
all these misrepresentations
that have been dreamed up
to explain what couldn't be seen?
I can see.
I hear.
I feel.
I taste.
I smell.
It's all I've ever done.
Why should I know
what isn't what is?

Why should a black cat
be different from a cat?
Without my name
would people still tell me
what I should know
or would they call me nameless
and let me out
Only at night?

OH AMERICA

Carnage. A complete sentence in a country at war with itself.

From the Valentine's Day heartland to the sea and the shining seas.

Spy balloons are a joke folks!
Why would any country be afraid of America?
We kill off our own!
Don't kid yourselves.
We aren't a threat to anyone but ourselves.

So now, sing a song, paint a picture, write a poem,
carve a face into a mountain
where your soul still shows its face.
The soul of America

Spirit children under the rubble just out of arms reach.

Oh, America!

RIDE THE THERMALS

There when time was a blip on the screen
of the sacred
And out of the way
The sky bowed down with a breath of
forever
The wind stayed out of the fray
Wings spread wide and circled ever higher
Where castles claimed to be passing
clouds
And hanging from the heavens bittersweet
remembrance
Like Spanish Moss shredded into shrouds

Ride Ride the Thermals
Ever higher, Ever higher, ride
Ride, Ride, Ride the Thermals
Masked marauders of the sky

Like a cloak someone wore in a make
believe dream
Brilliant as a drop of solid gold
The leaf that held the holy, scented the
story
Side-stepped misfortune and left it blood-
whipped old
"Caution," cried the thunder set back at a
siding
When the mention of it curled up all the
stars
Climb up a few more nightmares, release
the sudden poison
Come a little closer if you will tell us when
you are

Ride Ride the Thermals
Ever higher Ever higher, ride
Ride Ride Ride the Thermals
Masked marauders of the sky

ORDER OF THE CALENDAR

The calendar
hangs low
on the
brick.

The hidden nail
is filled
with dreams
of numerical
dust.

We see quiet
spaces a
whispering
pillow fans.

But are at a
loss to
discuss the
nature of
yesterday's
darker ink.

GOOD MORNING WIND

Good
morning
wind,
with
fire crackling
as
water
rises
above us,

invite
me in,

hold my
hand,
caress my
lips,

desperate
breaths
from an
avalanche covers each
century

close
the
cape,
adorn
volcanic earth
as lava
spews down
your breasts
and

keeps
our
warm
eyes
open
to the
waterfall's
roar

GRACEFUL AS SUN WARMS
for Silvia Scheibli

Graceful
Red Tail
takes twirls

through windows
in pine groves

trailed by caws
of
black crows

in blue
sky

while
jays
call

HOW PROUD, POOR PITIFUL AMERIKA

Poor pitiful Amerika,
But wait, it's not everyone,
everything,
it's only that where arms once were
now there are legs
& eyes have been replaced
by nostrils closed
& ears are absent &
in their places are mouths, lips
& teeth are twine
like a spider web of
magical mornings
made from forehead lines
& elbow grease
all aligned with heartbeats
heard where waves crash
cymbal-like under moonlit swords
& we listen with our tongues
while speaking languages
whose ancestors are wax & bone.

The brittle forecast is stone,
bright stone, but stone
nonetheless, childless
& emptiness & remember
the dance of the roosters death
head in hands, long black gowns
enemies above the border towns
changed names in cradles with crowns.

There was a string to pull
to light up the world
& one beside it

to keep us all warm.
Poor, pitiful Amerika
How happy can it be?
So smile and be done
with gloom like the Amerika
inside of trees, stand
& sing from insides out
the knowing that it's all about.

Celebrate jets that spray bomb
children in mother-made huts
full shawl & cardboard covers
to keep away the shivers,
the intoxicating flowers that
exchange power
in your teary-eyed hour
of mistaken sorrow,
it was only a comet, a meteor,
that moment was nothing
to write home about,
it was your life,
your sad
life Amerika
but don't take
my word for it
be as positive
as the
spirit will allow
as your sad soul
will disguise,
you see,
you are only
yourself,

no one else
Amerika,
no one else.

6

LITTLE BELL SERIES
INTERLUDE

from Armor Heart

…little bell, the messenger
listen to little bell,
listen to the quiet morning song

–Andrew Rosen

LITTLE BELL #4

Listen Little Bell.
To the quiet morning song
In your own dark heart
On a gray white sky
Between oak and pine

LITTLE BELL #7

Oh, Little bell, you are so still today.
I see yesterday's wind has untied your
Shoes & loosened scarves,
Removed your hat & gloves too.
Sun sparks oak tops to the south
Yet you must wait under boughs
For a cooler hour.

LITTLE BELL #8

Little Bell what brought the
red-tail hawk to your door?
The ancient candle flame
Burns branches
West of these brisk hours.
Thermals are quiet,
No movement can be seen in the leaves.
It is time to breathe and rest.

LITTLE BELL #9

The artificial light Little bell
brings you into focus.
While this hour
before dawn
ushers into place
southern skies,
waning stars
look to you for news
of home invasions,
bank robbery suspects,
weather systems coming out of
the Gulf and Pacific,
the final shot being made with
no time left on the clock,
unprecedented mass shootings
and my heart grieves
with you this morning, Little Bell,
over sadness in our world.

LITTLE BELL #12

Loosen your snowy white
   sleeves Little bell.

Let them drift
   into memories
  of a golden day.

Breathe that sacred breath.

LITTLE BELL #16

Come in from
   the cold Little bell.
Nothing I say will make
   you move.
Our hours cross paths in the
   last breath a musician takes.
His guitar and amplifier
   by his side.
Will the song you sing awaken
     lost sunsets from
        your dreams?
Can we count on Arctic
    conditions when we lower
        him into the ground?
The invitation is yours Little bell.
One step away from the light.
Baby what you want me to do?

LITTLE BELL #18

Little bell, on this crisp and breezy
   blue sky winter morning
   I hear your freedom song ring.
Your message to open eyes,
   hands, minds, and pores
   to the incitement of those serving injustices
   awakes warmer tones
   of this season.
The packed snow piled high
   and frozen water hanging low
   begin to create a new pathway.
Together they journey
   to the sea.

LITTLE BELL #20

It is so crisp and clear
  I thought you had fallen away
  Little bell.
You were gone.
You were invisible.
I jumped up in my chair.
I looked west to the trails
  of snow on the oak limbs and
    above the shed that's come
      back into view.
Twigs and pinecones were
  scattered over the yard
  from yesterday's wind.
Would this be the end
  of our days together?
It's been a lifetime full
  with blues, green, white,
  grays and brown.
I couldn't help to look again.
The chimes sang
  it's sweet refrain
  into the gentle morning breeze.

7

I hit the city and I lost my band

–Neil Young

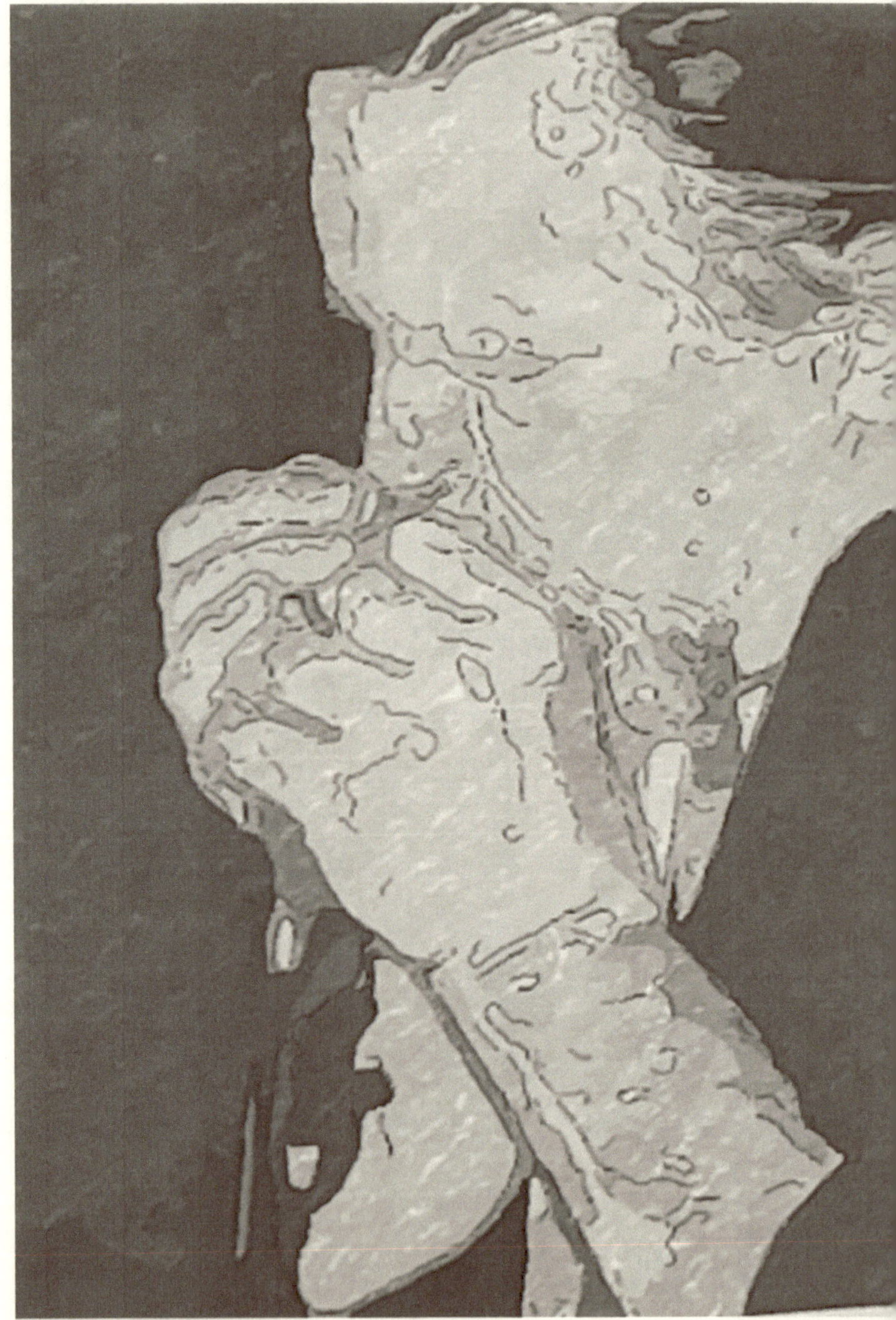

BABYLON

Frank Montresor
Stephen Sleboda

Cats look for bones
In a trashcan's supernova
Stretch 'n purr, pull their fur
Roll over 'n over
Umbrella woman takes the escalator
Up to Hell-o
Detour sign made her blind
And she straps her wheels to the fiery side

To the fiery side
To the fiery side
To the fiery side
To the fiery side

It's a three ring world
'neath a circus tent
Where caterpillars
Make lions dance
Foxtrot, cha-cha, jitterbug, jam
Take off their clothes
When they wanna stay warm
Grandma with horns
And her cotton candy kids
Dip their fingers in the water
Grandpa sits with machine guns tied
With machine guns tied
With machine guns tied

With machine guns tied
With machine guns tied
With machine guns tied
With machine guns tied

Two mythic figures
Zoomin' through Babylon
Knapsacks tied to the wind
Wind tied to the
Ringmaster's daughter
She screams
Let me out of Babylon
She screams
Let me out of Babylon
She wants out
Of Babylon

II.

Two mythic figures in a Fiero
Zoomin' through Babylon
Matriarchs step on patriarchs
Beside the walls of Babylon
Putrid brooks and evil women
Babble on in Babylon

Salamanders with yellow spots
Cause traffic jams in Babylon
Pollywogs in unlit windows
Chart the stars in Babylon
Protons and neutrons buzz 'round my head

Like clouds of black flies in Babylon
Looking into the slave driver's wagon
They closed my eyes in Babylon

After years of being high on ozone
I opened my eyes in Babylon
Flopping this way, flopping that way
My head's a windsock in Babylon
Poets and jesters fill the newsroom
Say the sooth in Babylon

III.

Pale horse with eight legs
Pulls the overture
Biplane skywrites
Trust us, trust us
Lamps and lanterns
Are filled with oil unholy
Fiero sticks like an arrow
In the belly
Of the Hall of Justice
I got cloud words
Piled up to my neck
Like the mythical purple hen
That pecks 'n pecks
Punching up the files of
All the dirty trials I
Drag my feet over broken tiles and
Every stinking mile further

Mama Sphinx
Breastfeeds a rent-a-cop
Elmer's glue
Threatnin' to put 'er claws
Through 'is head
If he does so much as move
But what's another corpse on
The pile of senseless, headless blue?

Wandering fluorescent aisles I
Skate down a lizard's smile
In a wizard's robe
Generic as a three-leaf clover

Is it better
To be a cop
In a dunce cap
watching the sun come up
In an all night coffee shop?
Give me a gun, give me a badge
Give me a remote control wife
And a body bag
Time to move, Moses
Maybe time to die
Water passes
Through the Pharoah's chariot
Moses decide

Who's suing who
And in which court room?
Would the village idiot care?
How 'bout the lady in the limo
with feathers, pearls and bleach blond hair?

IV.

Don't look
behind the crumbling walls of babylon,
Don't look
behind the closed doors in babylon,
Don't look, don't look
into the unmade beds in the babylon,
Don't look
behind the cracked mirrs in babylon,
into the broken wheels of babylon,
Don't look, don't look,
through the bob wire fence,
please don't look
behind the sun in babylon.

SOUND OF THE WORLD

Listen to the sound of the world
it's goin round and round

Round and round listen
to the sound of the world

The world goes round and round
listen to the sound

The people on the street are movin
to the beat of the underground sound

We're standin still yet we're movin
faster than the speed of light will

So grab a hold of that bolt of lightning
on the path as it passes by

Or catch a ride aboard the rainbow
and stretch across the morning sky

Lift your feet off the ground
Let the wings carry you on

Pull out the plug on the ocean
paint some new stars into the night

Grow some grass upon your head
and let the herd rest well tonight

CW JONES

CW Jones boards the subway
headed north, the new-old tie
looks Sci-Fi CentralPark.
Risin outta the dark,
a figure with mist for a heart
after one hard look
rolls a cold number down in the Ark.

Strip the rich from their jewels and
convince the wise to play fools, as a task
itself may take a lifetime or two.
Sing the song of the wind, then pretend it
ain't ever been and hold the coat of the
tramp through the sewer to bear the grin

CW Jones rides the daybreak into heat,
with another breath of life
frees colors in the rainbow knot
Bubbles burst in the air,
flags wave everywhere:
Do wars just end or is it
peacetime that makes life hot

Visit shrines in the sun, scalding water
warms the gun: Wear world like a
garment, loosen up everything.
Call to love is true, with violins for shoes,
walk on coals and let flames lite up the
strings.

CW Jones heads toward the sun going down,
Sci-Fi tie looks fine thru the window pane.
Glare thru grass is green with toxic
fumes obscene, the ride begins and
ends like some leap-frog dream.

Scatter off in the clouds wear rain like
blackened shrouds, wipe tears from her
cheek who went low when the river rose
A stitch to sew up the now, anytime,
anywhere, anyhow: This fortress of fear
with its fables goes rumblin on

CW Jones boards the subway headed home,
rainbow knot shines like Rockerfellow gold.
The dance floor and cat rest together on the track,
rollin to the station, rollin like it's never been told

Six o'clock or nine, the beginning or end of time,
white light holds each door where night slips in
Up and down the scale, with black notes
mist prevails, old tramp by his railing
says no to darkness as she slides in.

FULL OF BONES

I hear the lions den
Full of bones
It's what I hear
Full of bones
A man was left
Under the sun
It's what they say
It's what was done.

He seems around
Not in the cold
When it turns hot
He'll come around
They know he's more
Than ghost or man
Hear them say
The lions den

Winter waves, summer,
spring and fall
Just nod away, just nod away
Cloaks they wear, tear away
And bones they say,
take sun away,
take the sun away

Look at us that way
Under the stars
Shrieks we hear
Come from the night
The site aside a set of eyes
Too cold to see

Watch them move
Like flies through heat

It's what was said,
it's what was done
I hear them say the lions den
Shrieks we hear come from the night
Come from the night
come from the night
Come from the night

Furthur down
Cries forever
See the sound
Last gasp of summer
Nothing new
Under the sun
The order given
In the lions den

FALLING IN LOVE WITH A STATUE
for Deborah & Charlie

I think I'm falling in love with a statue
I don't want to look at myself
When I look in the mirror and see cold blank stares
Before I blink it all comes clear

I think I'm falling in love with a statue
Instead of taking a look at myself
I don't want to see the dart that pierces my liver
I don't want to see the bird that's caught in the snare

I think I'm falling in love with a statue
The Purple People Eater April Fool
If it's money I want - it's money I get
Like an oversized load in a hurricane

I think I'm falling in love with a statue
Perhaps this morning, maybe later toward noon
It's not a feeling; it's not emotion
It keeps me hungry, afraid and alone

I think I'm falling in love with a statue
My thoughts dress up and go out to play
I get to the tollbooth at the end of the road
The ticket always wants me to pay

I think I'm falling in love with a statue
It's made of marble and sweats in the rain
I'm tired and sore with nowhere to go
And I know it never will complain

That I'm falling in love with a statue
I don't want to look at myself

I'm falling in love with a statue
The mirror only shows one side

I tried talkin but the voice
in my head won't
listen to a word I say
Lady of the hours
Talking sunlight to the flowers
Keeps getting bigger every day

But I'm falling in love with a statue
And the mirror only shows one side
The clothes are black, the silver still shines
Excitement tends to run away and hide

Since I'm falling in love with a statue
Knowledge too wants to make itself scarce
Understanding with a shroud, comes in from out-of-bounds
Wisdom waits behind the spiral stair

Statue, statue, statue, statue,
Statue, statue, statue, statue
Fallin in love, fallin in love
Fallin in love with a statue

Statue, statue, statue, statue
Statue, statue, statue statue
Statue Ooo Ooo, Ooo Ooo, Ooo Ooo…

I know I'm falling in love with a statue
I know the mirror tells me so every day
I know I'm falling in love with a statue
And it's time to turn around and break away, break away, break away…

GRASS IS ALWAYS GREENER

Ernie Cox
Stephen Sleboda

The grass is always greener
on the other side of the road
The grass is always greener
on the other side of the road
Ever since my baby left me
That's where I call home

I was born on the south side
Sun shinin through my back door
I was born on the south side
Sun shinin through my back door
Ever since my baby left me
Sun don't shine here anymore

One and one is two,
two and two is four
Since my baby left me
Ain't counting on her anymore

The grass is always greener
on the other side of the road
The grass is always greener
on the other side of the road
Ever since my baby left me
That's where I call home

FIND SOMEONE IT MIGHT BE YOU

Who wants to wake up in a masquerade
Put on your boots, march down to the parade

Walk on, walk on, walk on around the corner
Find someone it might be you

Take it to the limit, take it all the way
Your coat, your hat, baby what you don't say

Walk on, walk on, walk on around the corner
Someone you find might be you

Parallel lines runnin' cross a cloudy sky
Indecent proposition with a twinkle in the eye
I gave to love the morning, and sat down by her side
The instant was gone, I couldn't keep from cryin

Walk on, walk on, walk on old horizon
Till you find the morning new(dew)

Beat up by the bus stop, go home & lick your wounds
That sound ain't the sun, it's crickets on the moon

Move on, move on, move on around the corner
That someone is in your way

Presidential election, caucuses & balloons
In the tunnel that's no light, it's champagne & buffoons

Move on, move on, move on around the corner
Do you even know you're in the way

She sat so sophisticated, legs crossed and all
He ran the streets till dawn, and met her by the wall
Rain came down the fifth day straight deep into withdrawl
He died that night in a pinstripe suit no coin to make a call

Move on, move on, move on sinister one
Until you see you're nothing new

The usual reception, tics, tights and wine
Bugged eyed computer talk about turpentine

Walk on, walk on, walk on around the corner
That person in the gutter might be you

It ended like it did, soldiers, cops and clay
Dust from the explosion made us look the other way

Walk on, walk on, walk on around the corner
Find someone it might be you

EDGE OF THE WORLD

I had thunder in my hair
Lightning round my waist
A hundred years ago
The canons took my place
Into the night
Coal black night
Long cold beautiful night

They'd turn the spotlights on
And set the hounds to howl
Old man sat on his old bones
With a frown about to scowl
Into the night
Coal black night
The long cold beautiful night

Wonder what I wore
I wonder what I said
Lit up like a funeral pyre
Ended up instead
Into the night
I died of fright
Coal black night
On the edge of the World

Believe I'm goin mad
Believe I'm turnin blue
Lion sleek as golden grass
Remembers me for you
Into the night
Coal black night
Long cold beautiful night

YOU SAW HIM SINGING

You would say you saw him
singing
Under red moon skies
Smoke from an old stogie
Made its way where he
changed disguise

Off Warren Wright Railway
A piercing eye from thermals above
Pick your poison made
With stench or lead
Like long ago a long lost love

With a whisper you wash the dishes
Or watch her hair hang down
But on the Miz'sippi Gambler
With no time to lose
You're gone to ground

Out-on the-long-way to-forever
No compass to find yourself
To get there, or go there, there
may be peace, maybe warfare
But what you find there, is
Your place to rest

Sorrow man stand on SUV
Flood waters run high
Without conviction or keys
Can he hold out till dawn
Or surrender his position to-be
Only-a-lie

Peaceday came early
Midnight starlight all around
All around where it is found

Side-roads-to rainy day heaven
Iceberg dreams fall-from
Scandinavian skies
Drink from goblets,
Porridge, foam & gruel where
Angry hearts choose your demise

SIR LEONARD

Black and White Houses for Eyes

> Frank Montresor
> Stephen Sleboda

Sing out swirling
Black
White House's
For eyes.
Tumble down crash site
Under overcast skies.
Blood-wind music, through
Dark night of the soul
Hour glass ocean
Screams out
Windows and doors.
Here comes red day
Dressed in threes
In the Brickville tunnels
Ventriloquists ease
Dreamscape roll your own
Galaxies.

Old Sir Leonard
Dactyls
Feather for stone
Ferryman's shadow
Into crosswalk alone.
Red carpet Someday
See a table inside
Quick cup of coffee
Write footprints for lines
Snakeskin blindfold
Know I should leave behind.

Grab hold of the
Flickering wall
Tapestry storm cloud
Slides cross the floor
Boat down dark river
Slips through the hands.

Deep blue skies
Deep blue in our heads
Off the dark
Onto the ledge
For all to hear
For all to see
The golden sword
Fields of green
The lady light
And brilliant scenes
The crooked path
Is all too clear.

Past coliseum drive
Straight into the light
The night she shines like
His darting feline eyes.
Two pieces maybe
Three, three pieces or more
Red line to Davis stop
American Spirit store
Son of emergency sing
'Cross the Queen of Swords.
But as the lion
Peacock sits with me
Dragonfly footbridge

Up beyond those trees
And that jeweled city
Is my destiny.

Dark wings pass
Falling bones
Of winter's light
On a path high above
The golden sword
Where Persephone
Is my bride
Beautiful nightmare
Delirious delight
See whose night's in air
Sir Leonard steps aside.

Porchfest banjo
Fuels
The dance with Mr. D
Somerville morning
Sun
Pyramid mind
Spy Pond's shore.
Gray reflection blurs
Down walking cobblestones
That old pipe burst
Paint runs down Java Joe's.
Read the boatman's eye
In a puddle on the floor
A cloak of mist clears
See us walking on the Prom.
You're the author,
You're the key

You gave me two coins
I know I'll need
And so begins your
Torch-lit odyssey.

Dim orange urn
Asleep in the valley
A healing breeze
Down by the sea
I heard his voice
Though his lips weren't moving
I heard Sir Leonard
Call the tune.

BUDDHA & THE BELLE

I was never so far away,
They were always by my side.
In the thunder and the lightning
Or on a midnight ride.
I never knew which one to pick
As she handed me each shell.
I couldn't help but play a trick
On the Buddha and the Belle.

On a weekend in December
The doctor met us at the door.
Next she said what she had to do
And if she had to, she could do more.
I didn't say a thing.
I was on vacation in Hell.
When I heard the cardinal sing
I saw the Buddha and the Belle.

The questions came real fast
Answers had to be found.
I remember one night lying on the floor.
And I couldn't even find the ground.
It was off to the magic bus,
Past the farmer in the dell.
When I saw there was no one left to trust
There was the Buddha & the Belle

Spring was just around the corner.
There was still snow near the fence.
It seemed like everything was working out,
But it never really made much sense.
I packed a bag and waved good bye

And caught a kiss down by the well.
"I thought I heard a baby cry,"
Said the Buddha to the Belle.

I came home late that evening.
There was quiet, water and ice.
I wrapped up in a blanket
And thought a song just might be nice.
A chorus came down from above
With nothing left to sell.
Some say luck, some say love
With the Buddha and the Belle.

Now there are hair ties on the table
And there's a bike out on the lawn.
I had to use the dictionary
To look up a familiar frown.
I just can't write the outcome.
I know it was a ladder that fell.
Even though they said you're welcome,
We never thanked the Buddha & the Belle.

MISTER SECRETS

Sweet dreams Mister Secrets
Sweet dreams pray tell
Sweet dreams Mister Secrets
Won't you sleep well

Take us on a journey
Take us on a trip
Cross the universe wide open
To a place I've never been

Sweet dreams Mister Secrets
Sweet dreams pray tell
Sweet dreams Mister Secrets
Won't you sleep well

Take us on a journey
Take us on a trip
Cross the universe wild and open
To a place I can't forget

HER BLESSINGS

She gave me her blessings,
it's something I never heard
She gave me her blessings
and it wasn't about the words
She wore no bright colors,
yet twinkled like the stars
and she wore no halo
but was seen from afar

When I went to the market,
was it to buy or to save?
While I tried to keep to myself,
there's a hand I saw wave
It had to come up close to my face,
or I surely would have passed by
It was gentle and soft to the touch,
like a place in my heart that won't die

She gave me her blessings,
it's something I never knew
She gave me her blessings
and by God's Grace I'll see it through
I'll swim to the mountains,
I'll climb unto the sea
I'll walk where the wild winds roar
wherever her blessings carry me, carry me,
carry me

MARY EILEEN

for Ann Marie Vanaria Sleboda

Mary Eileen, open your hand
We'll walk together over the sand
Mary Eileen, open your eyes to see
Whose arms you're in now
Mary Eileen, we'll be together somehow

Mary Eileen, child of the tides
Here before dawn, gone with the light
Mary Eileen, Queen of the song in my heart
That won't go away
Mary Eileen, we'll be together someday

Mary Eileen, I see your eyes
Blue like the ocean reflects in the sky
Mary Eileen, show us your smile
Know now how much we care
Mary Eileen, we'll be together somewhere

Mary Eileen, I hear your voice
Moving in circles over the noise
Mary Eileen, listen to hear songs of the quiet
Sounds of your song
Mary Eileen, we'll be together before long

OLD IRISH WOMAN

Alan Hurlburt
Stephen Sleboda

The chill of the wind is cold
The prayers in your heart are old
The old Irish woman prays the rosary

Her two sons have caught it
A foreigner may ask about it
The poor and the homeless
on the streets of America,

Puerto Rico, Ireland,
Iraq, Cuba and Africa
The truly oppressed know
when it raises its head

It's something in your soul
The rich cannot buy it
Education can't grasp it
Government can't control it
Ah, but her sons they have it
with Waltzing Matilda it's theme

The young in Australia have it
Mitch Snyder died for it
Tracy Chapman, Jim O'Leary sing with it
It's the gift that raises your consciousness
The language of the heart
Transcends wealth, religion and politics
Once you think you got it, it's gone

The old Irish woman says the rosary
Then she hums Waltzing Matilda

HERE COMES WINTERTIME
for Jack Corbin

Standin on the corner, standin in line
Fillin in the boxes, fillin out my time
Here comes a lady standin next to me
Sayin, "Don't have to worry cuz here comes the wintertime,"

Whoa, whoa don't ever know
Don't have to worry cuz
Here comes the wintertime
Whoa, whoa, don't ever know
Don't have to worry cuz
Here comes the rain and the snow.

Late November morning, overcast and gray
Traffic movin slower than
any words I gotta say
Here comes that big Mama
with a twinkle in her eye
Singin, "Don't have to worry cuz
Here come the rain and the snow."

Walkin down on Main St, walkin in the rain,
No money in my pockets
lookin for spare change
Here comes that doorway
with a woman standin there
Sayin, "Don't have to worry cuz
Here come the wintertime.

MOONLIGHT SERENADE
for Ned Nedski

Dancin' to a moonlight serenade

On the mountain where it's rained for thirteen days

Winding all about this countryside

Dreamin' like some freight train runnin' wild

Mysteries seem to fill the air we breathe

Where midnight packs her bags but never leaves

On the mountain where it's rained for thirteen days

Dancin' to a moonlight serenade

Centuries seem to line up like the stars

Take your partner swing around and 'round

Dancin' to a moonlight serenade

On the mountain where it's rained for thirteen days

STILL SING NOW

How can I think back now to more than ten years ago
When I set out on my own to nowhere and more
And the people I knew, they sat by the road
Just to say goodbye, just to say hello (hello)

There was a girl or two or three or four
Long John Silver and the corner store
In the sun setting rain, in the night every day
Inbetween the exits was a cold highway
(highway)

With a song I sang that I still sing now
And a junk I bought with a dead end job
I was heading down where I ain't been before
Was I going for peace, or was I going to war
(I don't know)

There were medical men and biology boys
Drunkards in alleys with pockets full of noise
Women walking high, feelin bad and lookin mean
Like masks you wear on Halloween (on
Halloween)

How can we still sing now about the people we know
The faces we see and the places we go
With this curse to wear like a scalding towel
When the sun won't shine where we still sing now (still sing now)

MENTAL INSTITUTION

Won't you come &
See me in the mental institution
Won't you come & see me today
Won't you come & see me in the institution
Won't you come and see me today
Come on now, come on down &
See me in the mental institution
Won't you come & see me carried away

I been lyin here for seven weeks
With four hundred people &
Not one of them speaks
It's not that I'm lonely,
It's just that I'm kinda sittin here alone
Won't you please come &
See me in the institution
Won't you come &
See me in the mental institution
It's not that I'm lonely, it's just I'm alone

I been stuck down here
For some kinda reason
And I don't know maybe
You can tell me what it's all about
Come on now, come &
See me in the institution
Visiting hours are twenty-four hours a day
Come on now, come on &
See me in this institution
Come on one of you people
Come & get off your high horse &
Pay your debt to society

That institution!

Come on down &
See me in the mental institution
Come on now, come on down,
You got nothin to hide
There's one man lyin on the floor,
He's been lyin there for seven years
Even the doctors don't know his name
Come on down maybe you can tell him
Come on down
See us in the mental Institution
Ya, maybe you'll learn how to play.

BOURGEOIS HEAVEN

i turned 69
in bourgeois heaven,
doing time
without a soul,
no one
could open my eyes but
the Immanentists tried,
the Immanentists tried.
The Immanentists tried
to show me better
while intuition
being denied
leaving
no one
but me
to blame cuz
the Immanentists
tried!

GREEN FROG SKIN GARDEN

give me a dollar, i'll pay you later
i'll see you later, alligator
i'd like to be stayin but i gotta be goin
i got something growin in my green frog skin garden

give me a minute, i'll take that dollar
i'll make you another - a hundred or two
and i'll keep on smilin though I might be lyin
i got something growing in my green frog skin garden

give me the change you don't give the beggar
i'll make the banks remember your number
and when you feel down, please consider this brother
i got something growing in my green frog skin garden

i don't give a hoot, a hip-hop or a hollar
don't flag me down with no almighty dollar
i'd like to be stayin and spendin my change here
but I got something growin in my green frog skin garden

so if you give of the time you spend with your dollars
your dollars will be spent by the time that you give
and it don't take much stayin - it don't take much goin
to know nothins growin in my green frog skin garden

VAGABOND VILLA

Jack Straw draws
His claws into the shape
Of a shadow you say you saw
Fenario footsteps
Follow you down
All the way down
To vagabond villa

On the way round
To cookie-crumb town
You watch all the palaces
A-tumbling down
Bertha's in the room
With the cripple and blind
I'd carry the cross
But it'd crack my spine

Bye we go, bye we go
Bye we go back
To vagabond villa

Hobo hops the freight
While law man waits
For chainsaw Charlie &
The funny smelling crate
Passengers thumb that
Twiddle-diddle-dee
While the crow
Blows the whistle
In time to agree

Racin & rockin
To lay me down
Cold mountain moment
Avoids the buryin ground

Past hilltop mansions &
The beach front homes
On this twelve lane highway
Where the Buffalo roamed
Not a word to say
With that freedom of speech
Wants to bring this place
Back within reach

CREDITS

Part 1: Epigraph by William Blake from *The Complete Poetry & Prose of William Blake*, page 37, edited by David Erdman. University of California Press, Berkeley Los Angeles London. 1965 1981 1982

Part 2: Epigrah by Pablo Neruda from *The Essential Neruda Selected Poems*, page 157, edited by Mark Eisner, City Lights Books, 2004

Part 3: Epigraph by Georg Trakl from *Twenty Poems of Georg Trakl,* page 21, translated and chosen by James Wright and Robert Bly, Sixties Press, Madison, Minnesota 1961

Part 4: Epigraph by Tomas Tranströmer from *Selected Poems 1954-1986*, page 145, Ecco Press, 1987, Robert Hass

Part 5: Epigraph by Rafael Alberti from *The Owls Insomnia*, page 37, Mark Strand, Atheneum, New York, 1973

Part 6: Epigraph by Andrew Rosen from *Armor Heart*, page 1, 2020

Part 7: Epigraph by Neil Young from "Harvest" from *Needle and the Damage Done*, Reprise Records, 1972

POET'S BIOGRAPHY

I grew up in middle class post WWII milltown Holyoke America. There was an explosion of children in Massachusetts filling up neighborhoods in those days from the 50s & 60s around Springdale, the Flats, South Holyoke, Churchill, Oakdale, Elmwood, Highlands, Bemis Heights, Woodmar Glen, Bray Park, Wycoff Park, Rock Valley, Smith's Ferry, Whiting Farms, Ingleside, Jarvis Heights, Downtown, and every other where up and down the mostly tree lined streets and alleys from the MtTom Range to the mighty Quinnehtukqut where dinosaur tracks still remain.

Go to college. That was the rallying cry. It just made sense if you could do it. Mrs Frost, our 5th grade teacher at Kirkland Elementary School, who read us Anne of Green Gables, left an unyielding impression on how far we could span the waves of our imaginations during those early reading class excursions developing our young and fragile sponge-filled unwavering neuropathways.

If you wanted to, you could ride away from a local car lot with a primer red Malibu for $500 bucks that would easily deposit you and a friend down JFK Boulevard into and under the whispy sprawling oaks & Spanish Moss of Plant Park circa University of Tampa 1975.

That was where Professor Duane Locke held residence and thank the universe and spirit forces that guided the decision-making map I spun blindfoldedly at our kitchen table on Magnolia Avenue like an offshoot of spin-the-bottle, that stopped nearer to Florida than California. California would have to wait for another lifetime. Another primal decision accomplished!

Enter the Immanentists; Dr. Locke's classes were about Silvia
Scheibli, Alan Britt, Jose Rodeiro, Steve Barfield, Nicomedes
Suarez, Charles P. Hayes, Paul B. Roth, Richard Collier, Garret
O'Sullivan, Fred Wolven and so many others weaving a tapestry of
souls including the parade of European poets from the 17th
century up and through the present day along with poets from vast
regions of the globe that only the Green Gables of Prince Edward
Island could hold for one sitting.

PUBLICATIONS BY STEPHEN SLEBODA

BOOKS

WHEN THE FOOTBRIDGE TURNS INTO THE
DRAGONFLY'S WING
Collective Copies Amherst, MA
2019 AccessRoadStudios

ON COLD MORNINGS
Endeavor Books
1999 PawPulsePress

WEDDING
UT Review
1979 Duane Locke

TWO THING THING POETS
Steve Sleboda and Connie May (Fowler)
UT Review
1977 Duane Locke

TESTIMONIALS

Stephen Sleboda's *I Cant Believe I Lived Wild & Raw* is the
embodiment of a robust, vigorous and empathetic muse whose
spirited voice lifts the reader energetically to a keen dimension
where the imagination surpasses reason by a long shot, as in "Ovens
of Uncertainty" where Sleboda tells us "The instant imagination
folded and became reason all hell broke loose." This innovative,
ground-breaking tone is heard throughout the poems as well as in
his trailblazing songs. "Vagabond Villa" states, I'd carry the cross /
But it'd crack my spine is the voice of someone who has battled
darkness, confronted terror and moved beyond it. The only thing
better than this Wild & Raw read is to hear his baritone voice
recite, "Green Frog Skin Garden" where he persuades us that, I
don't give a hoot, a hip-hop or a holler / don't flag me down with
no almighty dollar.

> – Silvia Scheibli, author of *In the House of Rain,*
>   Concrete Mist Press

In Sleboda's poetry, not only is anything possible, and breathtaking,
but surprise is probable. Directing a symphony of images, feelings
and textures, he invites us and sometimes pushes us into places we
wouldn't go without his insistence, and, ultimately, he gifts us with
freefalling gently through a world of unexpected beauty where
"thinking bursts into crumbs" and it becomes "easier to grow
feathers and pretend about a dream in an attic." We arrive changed,
and looking for more.

> – Liam Quirk, Songwriter, Writing & Rhetoric
>   Instructor, Rider University

Steve Sleboda is a long-standing Immanentist poet who utilizes nature as a referent and value base. There is an organic logic and clarity that encompasses his work. The author offers a hard-edge concrete image presenting an intuitively fresh perspective that is immediate to the senses. This enables easy access to the experience which is relaxed and seems almost conversational.

–Steve Barfield

Steve Sleboda's poems are like leaves floating down a stream. They ride the deep undercurrents of a life dedicated to the songs of the imagination to the solitary work in the living fields of the poems.

–Danny Shanahan
Author of *The Lotus Seed Poems*
(www.lotusseedpoetry.com)

I Can't Believe I Lived Wild & Raw explores the sacred and profane, the lived and the imagined, the desired, the attained, and the never-could-be. Stephen Sleboda is fully empowered in these poems: the artist at his most vulnerable, most authentic, and most magical. You'll catch whiffs of Federico Garcia Lorca and William Blake, yet every poem is unmistakably Sleboda. Learn of the moon and lost stars, summers of dust, lizard smiles, a green frog skin garden, and a mint trilled night that turns into a severed song. Imagery born from ash and bone burns these pages, setting fire to the darkness. And so does Sleboda's distinct syncopation. These poems are music, the songs of Sleboda's life, and like any good tune, you will whisper their rhythms and truths deep into the night.

> –Connie May Fowler, Author of *A Million Fragile Bones*, *How Clarissa Burden Learned to Fly*, *The Problem with Murmur Lee*, *Before Women Had Wings*, *Remembering Blue*, *When Katie Wakes*, *Sugar Cage*, and *River of Hidden Dreams*. Director: Vermont College of Fine Arts Novel Retreat and InkBlossom Writers' Conferences. Note: *Before Women Had Wings* is a 1997 American drama produced by Oprah Winfrey's Harpo Films as the first entry of the "Oprah Winfrey Presents" series and is the only film in the series in which Winfrey stars.

www.ingramcontent.com/pod-product-compliance
Lightning Source LLC
Chambersburg PA
CBHW022215050726
47590CB00002B/802